CONNECTIONS

Celebrating Cultures

by Liz Ray

Table of Contents

Different Cultures	2
Art	4
Music	7
Dance	10
Literature	13
Index	16

capstone
classroom

Different Cultures

As Americans we share the same homeland—the United States of America. We are all the same in many ways. But many of us have come from different backgrounds, or cultures. For example, immigrants who come here from other countries bring their customs with them. And Native American groups have their own traditions too.

Over time families pass their traditions on to their children and grandchildren. The traditions they share become part of their heritage.

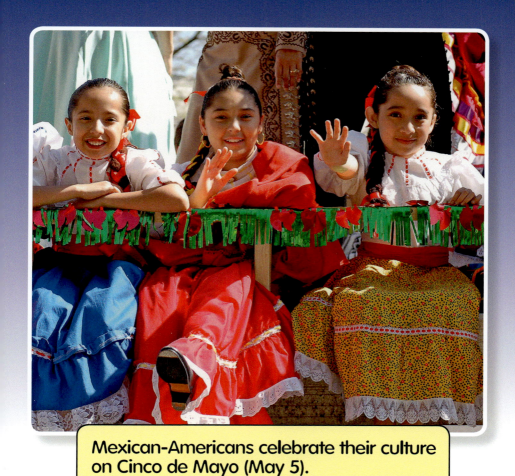

Mexican-Americans celebrate their culture on Cinco de Mayo (May 5).

Many people like sharing their traditions with other people. We can all enjoy traditions and customs from different cultures.

Art

Native Americans produce art that many people enjoy. Art is much more than just paintings and drawings. Art includes sculpture, weaving, pottery, and more.

Navajo weavers make beautiful, colorful rugs, blankets, and wall hangings. Their designs have been passed down for hundreds of years. Their weaving tradition is part of Navajo heritage.

part of a Navajo blanket

Native American pottery

Native American squash blossom necklace

A sculptor, weaver, or potter can make useful objects as well as lovely works of art.

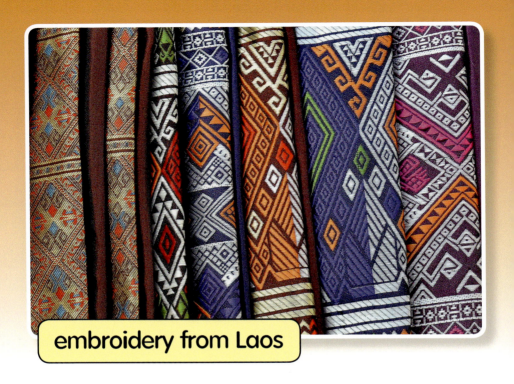

embroidery from Laos

Many women from Laos pass on a special tradition. They show others how to embroider clothing. They use colorful thread, and they count stitches carefully.

Music

All over the world, people sing, chant, and make music. Immigrants and visitors bring their music to the United States. This new music then becomes part of the American culture.

Many familiar songs today began in other countries. One such song is "Yankee Doodle." British soldiers may have brought this song here from England in the 1700s.

Sometimes brand new music comes from old songs. Jazz came from early African-American music, such as work songs and other songs called spirituals.

jazz concert

Many jazz musicians and singers still try to create new music. The musicians make up music together as they play their instruments.

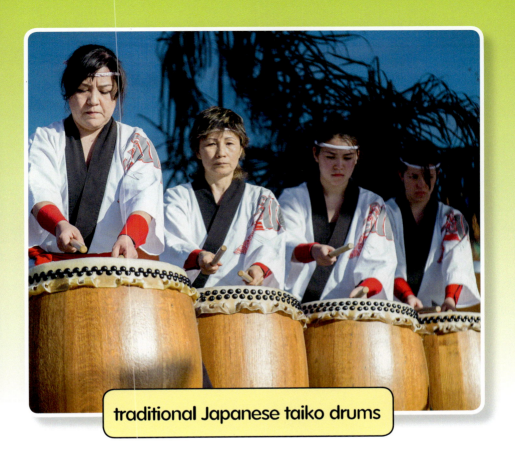

traditional Japanese taiko drums

Traditional music is often played at weddings and other celebrations. This is one way that people enjoy and pass on their musical heritage.

Dance

Along with music, dance is part of people's lives all over the world. Traditional dances are different from place to place. But most dances have something in common—the joy of movement!

In some dances the movements are fast and lively. For example, a lively dance that came from Poland is called the polka. In other types of dances, the movements may be made slowly.

A dancer can be like an actor and use movement to tell a story. Dances can also help celebrate special times in people's lives.

hula dance

The hula is an important dance in Hawaii. The dancers move to the music of traditional songs or chants. Each movement has a special meaning. The hula helps Hawaiians feel proud of their heritage.

Chinese lion dance

The lion dance is part of some Chinese celebrations in the United States and China. Dancers are inside the lions' heads and bodies. They dance to drums and are often followed by crowds.

Literature

The best of the world's stories, poems, folktales, and other kinds of writing are all part of literature. Many of today's most popular stories began long ago. People would tell each other stories, and then the stories would be told over and over again to other people. Over time writers would write down these stories.

Some stories may be similar in different countries. For example, the Cinderella story came from China. There are hundreds of retellings of this story all over the world.

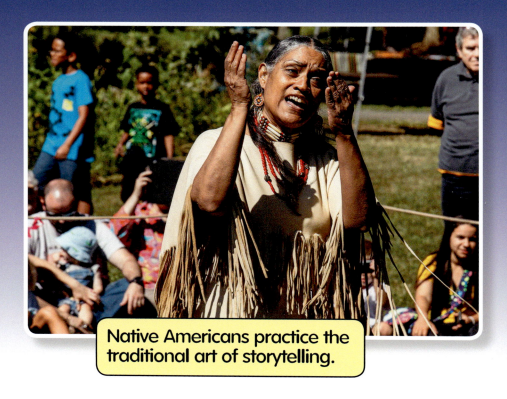

Native Americans practice the traditional art of storytelling.

People from many cultures tell stories about characters who play tricks. These stories are called trickster tales. In African stories Anansi the spider is a trickster. Coyote is known as a trickster in Native American tales.

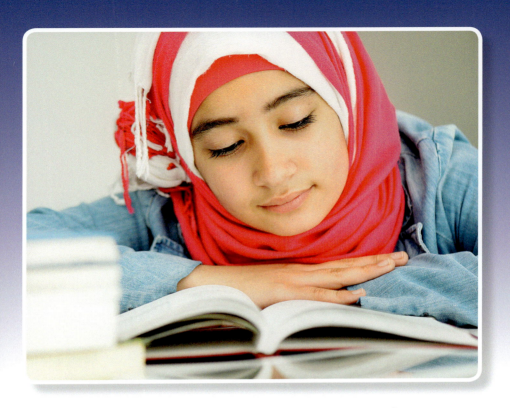

One way we can enjoy each other's heritage is through literature. Think about your own heritage. What special traditions make you feel happy or proud? Which ones would you like to share with others?

Index

art
    embroidery, 6
    Navajo weavers, 4
dances
    hulas, 11
    lion dances, 12
    polkas, 10
heritage, 2, 4, 9, 11, 15
Laos, 6

music
    jazz, 7, 8
    spirituals, 7
    "Yankee Doodle," 7
stories
    Cinderella story, 13
    literature, 13, 15
    trickster tales, 14
traditions, 2–4, 6, 15